Animal Diaries
Life Cycles

A Snake's Life

by
Ellen Lawrence

Consultants:

Suzy Gazlay, MA
Recipient, Presidential Award for Excellence in Science Teaching

Brian Hubbs
King snake Expert; www.mountainkingsnake.com

Kimberly Brenneman, PhD
National Institute for Early Education Research, Rutgers University, New Brunswick, New Jersey

BEARPORT
PUBLISHING

New York, New York

Credits

Cover, © Daniel Heuclin; 2, © Jason Mintzer/Shutterstock; 4, © Rob Marmion/Shutterstock; 5, © Design pics/Superstock; 6, © Steve Cukrov/Shutterstock; 7, © Bill Love/NHPA/Photoshot.com; 8, © Borhuah Chen/Shutterstock; 9, © Jim Merli/Visuals Unlimited/Science Photo Library; 10, © Roger Jones/Shutterstock; 10–11, © Danita Delimont/Getty Images; 12, © Jason Mintzer/Shutterstock; 13, © John Scharpen; 15, © Jim Merli/Corbis; 16–17, © Matt Jeppson/Shutterstock; 18, © Guenter Leitenbauer; 19, © Guenter Leitenbauer; 20, © Chris Mattison/FLPA; 21, © Daniel Heuclin/Naturepl; 22L, © Gary Nafis; 22R, © Matt Jeppson/Shutterstock; 23TL, © Borhuah Chen/Shutterstock; 23TC, © Roger Jones/Shutterstock; 23TR, © Tratong/Shutterstock; 23BL, © Danita Delimont/Getty Images; 23BR, © Evgeny Tomeev/Shutterstock.

Publisher: Kenn Goin
Senior Editor: Lisa Wiseman
Creative Director: Spencer Brinker
Design: Alix Wood
Editor: Mark J. Sachner
Photo Researcher: Ruby Tuesday Books Ltd.

Library of Congress Cataloging-in-Publication Data

Lawrence, Ellen, 1967–
   A snake's life / by Ellen Lawrence.
      p. cm. — (Animal diaries: Life cycles)
   Includes bibliographical references and index.
   ISBN-13: 978-1-61772-416-9 (library binding)
   ISBN-10: 1-61772-416-5 (library binding)
   1. Snakes—Life cycles—Juvenile literature. I. Title.
   QL666.O6L36 2012
   597.96—dc23
                          2011044730

For more information, write to Bearport Publishing Company, Inc., 45 West 21st Street, Suite 3B, New York, New York 10010. Printed in the United States of America in North Mankato, Minnesota.

10 9 8 7 6 5 4 3 2 1

Contents

Looking for Snakes..................4

Snake Eggs 6

The Babies Hatch 8

Tiny Kings............................10

A Scaly Skin 12

A New Skin! 14

A Sunbathing Snake 16

Rat for Supper 18

Waiting for Spring 20

Science Lab 22

Science Words 23

Index 24

Read More 24

Learn More Online 24

About the Author 24

Name: _Grace_   Date: _April 15_

Looking for Snakes

Uncle Joe

Grace

Today, I saw two ringed snakes in some bushes near my Uncle Joe's ranch.

He said they were California mountain king snakes.

Uncle Joe is a scientist who studies snakes.

I like to go looking for snakes with him on weekends.

He said the snakes were a male and a female that were meeting up to **mate**.

California mountain king snakes become adults and mate for the first time when they are about 2 feet (0.6 m) long.

California mountain
king snake

rings

Describe what a
California mountain
king snake looks like.

5

Date: June 17

Snake Eggs

Today, we found ten white king snake eggs hidden inside an old tree stump!

Uncle Joe says that female king snakes lay their eggs about 60 days after mating.

They lay the eggs in a secret place, such as inside a rotting log or under some rocks.

Female king snakes don't stay to protect their eggs after they have laid them.

These are life-size snake eggs.

tree stump

a snake laying an egg

eggs

Unlike a chicken egg, a snake egg doesn't have a hard shell. Instead, its shell feels like soft leather.

Why do you think the female king snake hides her eggs?

Date: **August 14**

The Babies Hatch

It's been about 60 days since the snake laid her eggs.

Today, Uncle Joe and I saw some tiny snakes begin to hatch from the eggs.

Sometimes raccoons, skunks, and other **predators** eat snake eggs.

That's why female snakes hide their eggs.

The tree stump was a good hiding place.

All the eggs stayed safe!

a snake hatching from an egg

Baby California mountain king snakes have the same red, black, and white rings as their parents.

eggshell

baby snake

Look carefully at the color pattern on the baby king snake in the picture above. Which one of the snakes on the right has the same pattern?

①
②
③

(The answer is on page 24.)

Tiny Kings

When baby king snakes hatch, they are about nine inches (23 cm) long.

From birth, the babies can take care of themselves.

They already know how to find food.

They also know to hide in cracks in rocks to stay safe from predators.

Animals such as owls and raccoons catch and eat baby snakes.

an owl eating a small snake

baby king snake

There are about 2,700 different kinds of snakes in the world. Some kinds lay eggs, while others give birth to live babies.

Look at the snake's skin. What do you think it feels like?

11

A Scaly Skin

Today, Uncle Joe carefully picked up one of the baby snakes.

I touched its skin.

It felt dry and smooth!

A snake's skin is covered with **scales**.

The scales are little folds of skin that overlap each other.

A snake's scales protect its skin as it slithers over rocks and rough ground.

Snakes don't have eyelids. They have a see-through scale that covers and protects each eye.

see-through scale

scales

baby king snake

Date: **September 1**

A New Skin!

It has been two weeks since the baby snakes hatched.

Today, we watched one of the babies wriggle out of its skin.

It took about four hours!

The baby snake's body had grown bigger, and its old skin was too tight.

Underneath the old skin was shiny new skin.

Most snakes shed, or lose, their skin several times a year. A snake sheds its skin when its body has grown bigger. It also sheds its skin if the skin gets hurt or worn out.

old skin

new skin

a scarlet king snake
shedding its skin

15

Date: <u>September 15</u>

A Sunbathing Snake

Early this morning I saw one of the baby king snakes lying in the sun.

Uncle Joe said the snake had gotten cold in the night.

It was using the sun to warm up its body.

Snakes are cold-blooded.

This means their body **temperature** goes down when the air is cold, and goes up when it gets warm.

Snakes belong to an animal group called **reptiles**. All reptiles are cold-blooded, and most lay eggs. Reptiles also have a backbone and scaly skin.

Date:  October 1

Rat for Supper

This evening Uncle Joe and I spotted a snake creeping up on a rat.

Suddenly, the snake grabbed the rat in its mouth and began to swallow it whole!

King snakes can open their mouths wide enough to fit in a meal that's bigger than their heads.

King snakes eat animals such as rats, mice, baby birds, and other snakes.

forked tongue

Snakes don't have noses. They can smell through their tongues! They flick their forked tongues in the air to smell for food.

rat

Date: **December 1**

Waiting for Spring

Winter has come, and the weather is getting colder.

Uncle Joe says the king snakes will spend the winter resting.

They will hide in underground holes or under piles of rocks.

When the weather warms up in spring, the adult snakes will be ready to mate again.

I can't wait to see more snakes in the spring!

a snake looking for a winter sleeping spot

California mountain king snakes may live for more than 20 years!

An adult California mountain king snake can be up to 47 inches (119 cm) long. Measure a piece of string to this length. Lie down next to the string. Is the snake longer or shorter than you?

21

Science Lab

Snake scientists can use a snake's pattern, or markings, to figure out what type of snake it is.

If you look <u>quickly</u>, many types of snakes look alike.

Arizona coral snake

California mountain king snake

If you look <u>carefully</u>, however, you will see differences in their body markings.

Snake scientists learn to become good observers—and you can too.

Look at each of these patterns.

Figure out what color or colors are missing from each one.

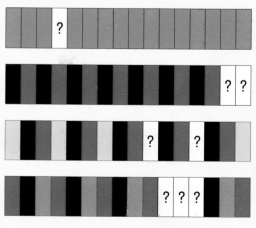

(The answer to this activity is on page 24.)

22

Science Words

mate (MAYT)
to come together to
produce young

predators (PRED-uh-turz)
animals that hunt and kill
other animals for food

reptiles (REP-tilez)
cold-blooded animals,
such as snakes, lizards,
and turtles, that have dry,
scaly skin, a backbone,
and lungs for breathing

scales (SKALEZ) small pieces
of hard skin that cover the
body of a snake

temperature
(TEMP-pur-uh-chur)
a measurement of how
hot or cold something is

Index

baby snakes 8–9, 10–11, 12–13, 14, 16

backbones 17

body temperature 16–17

cold-blooded 16–17

eggs 6–7, 8–9, 11, 17

eyelids 12

feeding 10, 18–19

hatching 8, 10, 14

hunting 10, 18

mating 4, 6, 20

patterns 9, 22

predators 8, 10

reptiles 17

rings 4–5, 8

scales 12

shedding 14–15

skin 11, 12, 14–15, 17

tongues 18

venom 22

Read More

Hughes, Monica. *Scary Snakes (I Love Reading).* New York: Bearport Publishing Company (2006).

Stewart, Melissa. *Snakes! (National Geographic Readers).* Washington, D.C.: National Geographic Children's Books (2009).

Wilsdon, Christina. *Snakes (Amazing Animals).* New York: Gareth Stevens (2009).

Learn More Online

To learn more about snakes, visit **www.bearportpublishing.com/AnimalDiaries**

Answers

Correct snake pattern from page 9

②

Correct patterns from page 22

About the Author

Ellen Lawrence lives in the United Kingdom. Her favorite books to write are those about animals. In fact, the first book Ellen bought for herself, when she was six years old, was the story of a gorilla named Patty Cake that was born in New York's Central Park Zoo.